FAMOUS AMERICAN LANDMARKS

THE WHITE HOUSE

HOME OF THE FIRST FAMILY

KATHRYN WALTON

PowerKiDS press™

New York

Published in 2023 by The Rosen Publishing Group, Inc.
29 East 21st Street, New York, NY 10010

First Edition

Editor: Natalie Humphrey
Designer: Michael Flynn

Photo Credits: Cover Orthan Cam/Shutterstock.com; series background lukbar/Shutterstock.com; p. 4 Rich Crable Photography/Shutterstock.com; p. 5 Sergiy Palamarchuk/Shutterstock.com; p. 7 Everett Collection/Shutterstock.com; p. 9 https://en.wikipedia.org/wiki/File:Gilbert_Stuart_Williamstown_Portrait_of_George_Washington.jpg; p. 11 (James Madison) https://commons.wikimedia.org/wiki/File:James_Madison(cropped)(c).jpg; p. 11 (map) https://commons.wikimedia.org/wiki/File:Washington_DC_1794-.jpg; p. 13 (drawing) courtesy of White House Historical Association; p. 13 (James Hoban) https://commons.wikimedia.org/wiki/File:James_Hoban_circa_1800_-_Crop.jpg; p. 15 Tish11/Shutterstock.com; p. 17 (stable) courtesy of the Library of Congress; p. 17 (Thomas Jefferson) https://commons.wikimedia.org/wiki/File:Official_Presidential_portrait_of_Thomas_Jefferson_(by_Rembrandt_Peale,_1800)(cropped).jpg; p. 18 https://commons.wikimedia.org/wiki/File:Flickr_-_USCapitol_-_British_Burn_the_Capitol,_1814.jpg; p. 19 https://commons.wikimedia.org/wiki/File:The_President%27s_House_by_George_Munger,_1814-1815_-_Crop.jpg; p. 21 (White House) ESB Professional/Shutterstock.com; p. 21 (wedding) https://commons.wikimedia.org/wiki/File:Nugent%E2%80%93Johnson_wedding_cph.3a00694.jpg.

Cataloging-in-Publication Data

Names: Walton, Kathryn.
Title: The White House: home of the first family / Kathryn Walton.
Description: New York : PowerKids Press, 2023. | Series: Famous American landmarks | Includes glossary and index.
Identifiers: ISBN 9781538387290 (pbk.) | ISBN 9781538387313 (library bound) | ISBN 9781538387306 (6pack) | ISBN 9781538387320 (ebook)
Subjects: LCSH: White House (Washington, D.C.)-Juvenile literature. | Washington (D.C.)-Buildings, structures, etc.-Juvenile literature.
Classification: LCC F204.W5 W348 2023 | DDC .975.3-dc23

Manufactured in the United States of America

CPSIA Compliance Information: Batch #CSPK23. For Further Information contact Rosen Publishing, New York, New York at 1-800-237-9932.

Find us on

CONTENTS

THE PRESIDENTIAL HOME

The White House has become one of the most famous landmarks in the United States. The White House is the home of the United States executive branch. This includes the president, their advisors, and other departments. After it was built starting in 1792, each president held meetings, met with officials, and lived in the halls of the White House.

★ LANDMARK FACTS! ★

The White House was first officially called the "White House" by President Theodore Roosevelt in 1901. Before it was officially known as the White House, it was also called the "President's palace," the "President's House," and the "Executive Mansion."

Throughout its over 200-year history, the White House has told the story of the American people and their struggle for freedom and **sovereignty**. From the moment the first **cornerstone** was laid in 1792 until today, history has been made in the White House each day.

THE BIRTH OF A NEW NATION

Unhappy with their treatment by the British, the American colonies fought back. On April 19, 1775, the American Revolution began. This war lasted nearly seven years. After a hard fight, the United States won. In 1783, the British and the Americans signed the Treaty of Paris, finally ending the war.

But the battle of creating a new nation had just started. Now that the Americans had their freedom, it was time to decide how their new nation would be run. On September 17, 1787 the **Constitution** was signed, outlining a divide of power to keep the government from becoming just like a British **monarch**.

THE FIRST PAGE OF THE TREATY OF PARIS PROMISES AN END TO FIGHTING AND PEACE BETWEEN GREAT BRITAIN AND THE UNITED STATES OF AMERICA.

Original Definitive Treaty
3 Sept. 1783

In the Name of the most
Holy & undivided Trinity.

It having pleased the divine Pro-
vidence to dispose the Hearts of the most
Serene and most Potent Prince George the
third, by the Grace of God, King of Great
Britain, France & Ireland, Defender of
the Faith, Duke of Brunswick and
Lunebourg, Arch Treasurer and Pr
Elector of the Holy Roman Empire &c..
and of the United States of Amer.
to forget all past Misunderstandings and
Differences that have unhappily interrup
ted the good Correspondence and Friendship
which they mutually wish to restore;
to establish such a beneficial and satisfac
tory Intercourse between the two Countr
upon the Ground of reciprocal Advantag
and mutual Convenience as may p
and secure perpetual Peace & Harmon

7

CHECKS AND BALANCES

The Constitution outlines the roles and powers of three separate branches of government: the executive branch which leads the country and enforces laws, the judicial branch judges if laws follow the Constitution, and the legislative branch creates and passes laws. These branches share power to make sure no branch becomes too powerful. This is called a system of checks and balances.

In 1789, George Washington was elected the first president of the United States, despite not truly wanting the role. Knowing he was laying the groundwork for presidents to come, President Washington had a lot of work to do.

★ LANDMARK FACTS! ★

The presidential family is also called the first family. The president's wife is called the first lady and their children are called the first children.

GEORGE WASHINGTON IS THE ONLY PRESIDENT TO WIN EVERY **ELECTORAL VOTE**.

9

CRAFTING D.C.

In 1790, Congress passed the Residence Act. This act established a new federal district along the Potomac River that would serve as the central location for the U.S. government. President Washington chose the exact location on land Maryland and Virginia then ceded, or gave up, to create the capital city. The **commissioners** of the new district named it Washington, D.C. in honor of President Washington.

The original plans for the city itself were **drafted** by Pierre Charles L'Enfant, a French **architect** and designer. In 1791, President Washington hired L'Enfant to create the layout for Washington, D.C., as well as other government buildings.

THIS FEDERAL DISTRICT WOULD NOT BE PART OF ANY STATE BECAUSE FOUNDING FATHER JAMES MADISON WORRIED A STATE WITH THE CAPITAL WOULD BECOME TOO POWERFUL.

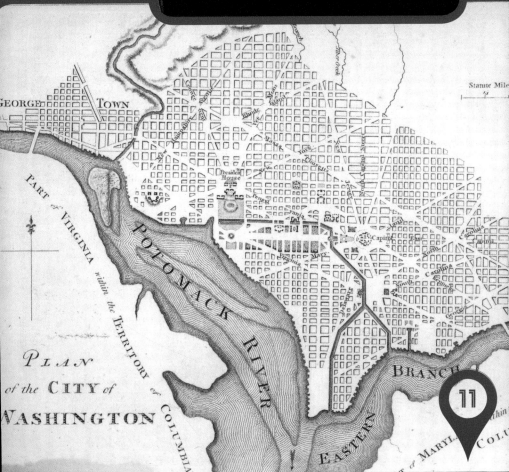

JAMES MADISON

JAMES HOBAN STEPS IN

While most of L'Enfant's original plan for the city was followed, L'Enfant was difficult, or challenging, for the commissioners to work with. He was later fired from his position, and the government leaders set out to find replacements.

For the president's home, President Washington had someone in mind. After seeing his work in South Carolina, Washington found Irish builder and architect James Hoban. After winning a contest for his plan, Hoban was selected as the builder for the president's home. These plans were inspired by Leinster House in Dublin, Ireland.

★ LANDMARK FACTS! ★

The White House wasn't the only building that James Hoban worked on after he moved from Ireland to the United States. He was also one of the many architects who oversaw the building of the Capitol.

JAMES HOBAN

WHO BUILT THE WHITE HOUSE?

In 1792, construction on the White House began, but help was in short supply. The commissioners of Washington, D.C. had originally planned to bring workers over from Europe, but couldn't get all of the help that they needed. Instead, the work was done by paid laborers, skilled craftsmen, and enslaved people.

As the U.S. government itself didn't hold enslaved people, slave owners were paid to let the government hire them. Enslaved people were taught to work in the government's **quarry** and were required to mine the stone used to build the White House. They also worked alongside paid **masons**.

★ LANDMARK FACTS! ★

Though George Washington oversaw the construction of the White House, he never actually lived in it. Instead, George Washington lived in a home in Philadelphia, Pennsylvania called The President's House. At the time, Philadelphia was the nation's capital.

14

WHERE IS THE WHITE HOUSE?

WASHINGTON, D.C.

THE WHITE HOUSE

PENNSYLVANIA AVENUE

CAPITOL

POTOMAC RIVER

THE WHITE HOUSE IS LOCATED AT 1600 PENNSYLVANIA AVENUE N.W. IN WASHINGTON, D.C.

A MUSEUM IN THE WHITE HOUSE

By the time the White House was close to finished, there was a new president. John Adams, the second president of the United States, moved into the White House on November 1, 1800. Adams only lived in the presidential estate for five months before he was replaced by Thomas Jefferson.

In 1801, Jefferson created the White House Museum in the front entrance hall of the White House and opened the doors to the public. The museum showed **artifacts** from Lewis and Clark, two American explorers, to tell the public about the mysterious and unsettled western United States. The collection included arrowheads, animal skins, and even two live grizzly bear cubs!

★ LANDMARK FACTS! ★

Meriwether Lewis and William Clark were two former soldiers hired by Thomas Jefferson to explore the Louisiana Purchase. This large territory that stretched over most of the Midwest was purchased from France in 1803.

BETWEEN 1802 AND 1803, JEFFERSON COMPLETED A PLAN FOR A CARRIAGE PATH AND STABLES ON THE WHITE HOUSE GROUNDS.

THOMAS JEFFERSON

THE WAR OF 1812

After serving two terms in office, Thomas Jefferson was replaced by James Madison. Madison was the first president of the United States during a time of war. After the attack of an American ship by the British, most of the U.S. Congress urged the president to start a war. On June 18, 1812, James Madison declared war against the British.

GOVERNMENT BUILDINGS BURNED. SOME GOVERNMENT OFFICIALS WANTED TO MOVE THE CAPITAL TO A NEW CITY TO SAVE MONEY.

In 1814, a large number of British troops captured Washington, D.C. On August 24, they began burning government buildings, including setting fire to the White House. The fire was so large it could be seen from 50 miles (80.5 km) away.

REBUILDING THE WHITE HOUSE

On December 24, 1814, the United States and British representatives signed a treaty to end the War of 1812. Soon after, James Hoban was brought back to rebuild the White House. Since so much damage was done by the fire, Hoban had to start nearly from scratch. In 1817, work was finished, and James Madison returned to the White House with his wife, Dolley Madison.

In the years that followed, each president added more and more to the White House. Just like the country itself, the White House is a symbol, or model, of many people **unified** as one.

★ LANDMARK FACTS! ★

The White House has just about anything a person could want. This 55,000 square foot (5,109.7 square meter) home has six different main floors with a two-floor basement. In total, there are 132 rooms, with 16 reserved for the first family, and 35 bathrooms.

EIGHTEEN WEDDINGS HOSTED BY PRESIDENTS AND FIRST LADIES HAVE TAKEN PLACE AT THE WHITE HOUSE.

GLOSSARY

architect: A person who designs buildings.

artifact: Something made by humans in the past that still exists.

commissioner: An officer in charge of a public service department.

constitution: The basic laws by which a country or state is governed. The U.S. Constitution is the piece of writing that states the laws of the United States.

cornerstone: A stone laid by builders at the corner of a building that often shows the date it was laid.

draft: An early version of a piece of writing. Also, to put something into written form.

electoral vote: The votes by a body of 538 electors who cast votes to elect the president and vice president.

masons: Someone who is trained to work and build with stone, concrete, or brick.

monarch: The king or queen that rules a country.

quarry: A place where large amounts of rock or stone are taken out of the ground.

sovereignty: The right to self-government.

unified: The state of being in full agreement.

FOR MORE INFORMATION

BOOKS

Krekelberg, Alyssa. *Astro the Alien Visits the White House*. Fairport, NY: Norwood House Press, 2023.

Taylor, Charlotte. *The Truth about the Founding Fathers*. New York, NY: Enslow Publishing, 2023.

WEBSITES

Kids Discover
kidsdiscover.com/quick-reads/weird-things-didnt-know-white-house/
Check out more interesting and weird facts about the White House.

White House History
www.whitehousehistory.org/tour-the-white-house-in-360-degrees
Take a virtual tour of the White House.

INDEX